Of Love, Life, and Journeys

WANDA ST. HILAIRE

SECOND EDITION

Of Love, Life, and Journeys
Second edition
Copyright © Wanda St. Hilaire, 2004–2019

All rights reserved. No part of this publication may be reproduced, stored in, or introduced into a retrieval system, or transmitted in any form, or by any means without the prior written permission of the author.

ISBN-13: 978-1-8943 3 1-17-3

Destinations Extraordinaire
Calgary, Alberta, Canada
destinoex@aol.com
www.wandasthilaire.com

Book design: Wanda St. Hilaire
Book layout: Ryan Fitzgerald

These poems are dedicated to all of the
world's women ...
for the incredible strength,
courage,
and beauty
we all silently carry.

Nothing else counts in this life

if our heart knows not the song of love

generously scattered

over all we touch

After the storm

the sun is strong and warm
and I am ice
the world is lush and verdant
and I am a desert
roses surround me
and I am a thistle
the moon is full and bright
and I
     am empty

*This moment
this kiss
sweeter than any nectar
is forever etched
into the memory of the Universe*

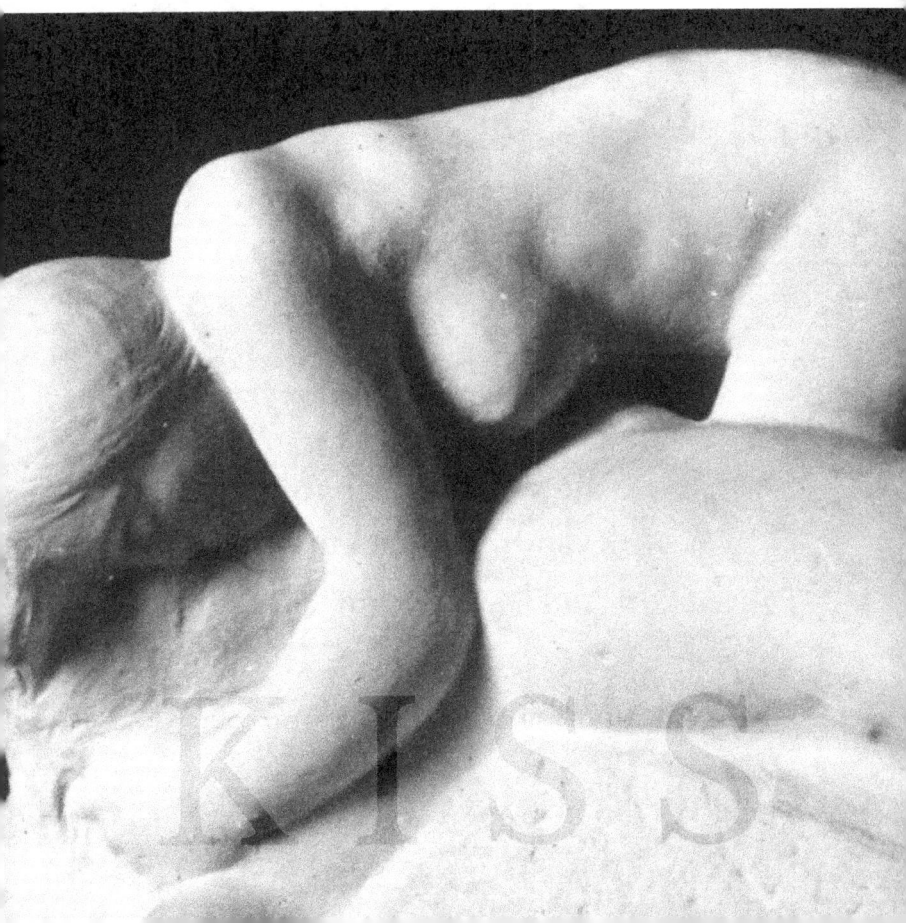

4

Grant me the courage

to accept this path
with all its peaks and valleys
and to see that all
is exactly
as the Universe has planned it.

A song

A beautiful crystalline voice
Words that embrace me
warm me
fill me when love is absent

A song is my lover

In your arms
my soul possessed an unbeknownst smile
Euphoria swam through my body
kissing all it passed
Like glass
hitting marble
was my heart
each cell of my being
   confused
      curling
to deflect the assault
Lost in no dimension
a fog of agony
   pressing
      pushing
upon your deception

Walk away from tyrants who suppress and belittle
never look back
for they have lost their way
and are as lethal to the human spirit
as a toxin is
to the tender earth

8

A woman's love
holds tendernesses so very sweet
Support like that of an ancient column
which remains through all
Her desires can feed your soul
So precious are the butterflies in her
as she watches you sleep
Few men stop to smell this essence
of a woman
absorbed in shallow pursuits
distracted by glimpses of glitter
never to know that which far surpasses
all worldly riches

Sueños

My mind floats on a hundred silk pillows
covered in honey kisses
golden streams of icy champagne
as I dream of a dark, indulgent lover
I cannot deny I have the soul of Cleopatra

My journeys to foreign soils
fill me with effervescent anticipation
To watch animated debates
over cappuccino in a café
To hear children sing
in a language I cannot understand
To savor good food
and fine wine
This is an education
of life and of passion
and for acceptance
to see that we are all neighbors
on this
our small planet

Mykonos
White-washed, sun-kissed houses
The presence of ghosts from centuries past
roam your narrow streets
your people steeped in tradition and history
you are a precious jewel of the Mediterranean

Touch is the essence which nurtures our souls

No matter our age or destiny in this life

I know not why or where they come from
these excruciating physical maladies

from my inner torment?
grief for unrequited loves?
bruises to my naïve heart?
injustices my consciousness
or unconsciousness
cannot accept?
or is it solely my divine fate
agreed upon
before my conception
for my time on Earth?

Please look into my eyes
listen to me
be here with me
not off on a future errand or endeavor
for this moment is now
and will never happen
again

Caresses and whispers
that transform us
to femininity and beauty
delicious freedom
when the arms of love and protection
encompass us
a song that transports us
 to the place of lovemaking
a murmured endearment
with a strong embrace
pulling us close in the night
are but a few
of our favorite things

Lovemaking

Does an angel wait nearby when you neglect her?
Or does she dissipate into the clouds to rest
with other celestial creatures
until she hears you call?

This I would like to know when my heart is mute
for I want not for her to lose me
in the murmurs of mortals
but to remain
in faith of my faith

You don't have the right.
You lust,
then spill waterfalls of I love you's,
covering everything in a mist of illusion.

You have only seen the shoreline of my ocean;
my storms are short, but tempestuous,
yet my lust does not wane.
I bruise, disappointingly frail and fragile,
but my lavender kisses will not die.

You will fear my appetites,
and my insolence is innate,
but when I dream,
the world is my smiling oyster.

My feline capacity for self-indulgence
may incense you,
and the depth of the lake that holds my tears
is unknown,
but when watered,
my love yields incandescent blossoms
of every colour.

After you have sailed these waters,
and time has told on you,
only then
        is the privilege
                yours.

As I travel alone
on unplanned adventures
sitting
   observing
      breathtaking scenes
etched eternally in my mind
when the notion of time is elusive
the gypsy in my soul
tells me home
is anywhere I am

Her eyes
they will giggle at you
and reveal her rising lust
seducing your senses

they flash in anger
and mist in the pain of harsh words
as they pledge her loyalty
they will stun you with their force
Look at them
for they are life

*Open your eyes
wake from your dreams
and remind yourself that today
you will heighten your senses
to each kindness shown
to every smile
all things beautiful
vast or tiny
for none of these gifts are insignificant
in the eyes of the Universe
or the core of your soul*

Where do the hearts of men hide
that comprehend the fragile beauty
of a woman's deepest being
and treat it
with its deserved reverence?

Living in a state of grace
is my highest aspiration.
To hold the aura of serenity
that beautiful heroines of the world possess ...
to offer all I meet the gift of truly listening ...
to handle life's challenges calmly ...
to taste, to smell, to savor the moment ...
to smile, to laugh, to touch ...
to leave behind me
a blanket of love,
warmth,
and light.

23

The innocence
of child and beast
is divine creation
placed here
for our unconditional love
and protection

24

They are music in the
wind, your words
delicious and sweet
But promise me nothing
For I have no place
to keep your broken ones

Ma Petite Soeur

How fortunate I am
to have been bestowed a beautiful sister
with a unique gentleness
and boundless patience
who believes in me
Her unconditional love is mine
through delirious happiness
and intense sorrow
My best friend always

Bring with you on your journeys

**AN OPEN MIND
FOR THE PEOPLE
 THEIR TRADITIONS
  THEIR LANGUAGE
AND THE COLORFUL SHADES OF THEIR LIVES
REVERE AND RESPECT THE LAND, THE SEA,
AND THE HOME OF OTHERS**

27

Each loss
has created small chips and fine cracks
heart and soul
But this loss has redefined the outline
altered the contents that dwell within

28

YOUR SCENT
  YOUR TASTE
    YOUR TOUCH

IT IS NONSENSICAL
THIS PRIMAL ENERGY YOU INVOKE
CAUSING MY UNIVERSE
TO COLLAPSE

The sea is my recovery
the smiles of strangers mend my broken soul
the winds wash away the melancholy
pebble by pebble
the sun's healing warmth dilutes the darkness
to the color of light

A spoken word
is power incarnate
it can intoxicate us with its headiness
resuscitate a drowning ego
or eradicate all past tendernesses
in but a moment
throw them not carelessly
for they could tear
the delicate fabric of a heart
or elicit a wound
never to heal
never forgotten

In his new daughter's eyes

I SEE THE PUREST OF LOVE
AS SHE GAZES UP AT HIM
AND HE DOWN AT HER
SURELY THE MOST PROFOUND
AND UNCLUTTERED
OF LOVE KNOWN

ICEMEN

Cold insinuating stares
they starve us of tender smiles,
of playful lust.
Leaning, sipping, with cool facades,
they wait, and watch,
selecting their prey for night's end.

I live in a land of extinct passion;
a lost art.
How did they get here,
all these Icemen?

Rushing and running,
confused little beings
scurrying,
caught in a maze.
Schedules, deadlines, obligations.
Furrowed brows and migraines.
Tempers stretched; igniting.
Futile obscenities screamed in traffic.

How bewildered God must be,
as He watches us dash past
love,
truth,
and beauty.

If I float freely down this river
rather than struggle against the current
the journey becomes that much easier
and the thrill of discovery
unfolds itself
bit by precious bit

If the shell of a heart hardens
to the unfairness and injustices dealt it,
does it sever the lifeline
that nourishes the beauty
and tenderness that live inside?
To carry a jaded and cynical heart
seems a most heavy and sad burden.
May we survive these trials,
only to become more resilient

yet still full of love and buoyancy

A lazy cat napping on the sofa in the galeria
A stray dog approaching, head down,
tail swaying in an anticipated touch
The rooster that knows not the hands of the clock
The unexpected play of dolphins
breaking the skin of the sea

This is the melody of Mexican life

Celebrate

the curve of her back
the swell of her belly
the rhythm of her sleep
all that she offers
and that which she aspires to be
for in her uniqueness
is perfection

This time that I have been granted
to listen to my heart
tells me all its secrets
reveals its desires
hidden in shadowed curves
opens the doors of my imagination
germinates seeds of generosity
and heightens my senses
to the surrounding beauty

Stop
Listen

**and these gifts
shall too be yours**

When the barriers of judgement are down
and our love escapes it cage

good things happen

*It is too easy to close my eyes
to taste you
breathe you into me
feel the warm yield of your mouth
I could fall into the belief that it was real
that you will hear me calling*

A full blue moon over the castillo
the last night of our foreign love
"Think of me always on a full moon."
And now I fear it will remain so
every month
of my life

42

the sun
its warmth
its strength
is slowly erasing the clouds you placed
with no remorse
for the storms you brought

An embrace ...
can water a wilting spirit
A kiss ...
can spark a long-dormant fire
A touch ...
can send shivers of unexpected warmth
straight to the soul
A small kindness ...
can transcend despair

Why then
do we pass these oases
in the deserts of out lives?

The thoughts of others
are not you
but the thoughts you hold
become who you are

   Do not batter the child within you
   for she weeps with each blow

Dwell on your goodness
     Bask in your courage
         See the lush spectrum
            of wildflowers you sow

                      over all you touch

I fear this jungle
For I know not whether
with the turn of a leaf
I will find a deadly poisonous snake

or an exquisitely
beautiful
butterfly

A formidable courage resides inside you
The path to your dreams is sometimes treacherous
But cast aside the shroud of skepticism
Ask your imagination for the stepping stones
to your aspirations

You have but one fleeting moment here with two choices:
The dark imprisonment of I can't
   or
       the enchantment of ...

I can.

A tiny light

far out in the swells of the sea
and suddenly
a wave
decimating it

Wait for it
Count on it
It will return

It wants to find you

Imaginary fences made of stone
can be dissolved with the power of thought.
'Shoulds' and 'Musts' and 'Have Tos', like dust,
can be carried away in the winds of change.
Shun boredom of the spirit—

Build sand skyscrapers ...
Ride wild horses through canyons ...
Meditate with monks in Katmandu ...
Eat colossal sundaes for breakfast ...
Sing sonnets with gondoliers ...
Run with bulls in Pamplona ...
Fly to the west side of the moon ...

Choice, a most neglected gift,
was given to you,
to me,
to all.

Your heart is a Mona Lisa
Why give it to petty thieves
who cannot decipher the
difference between an imitation
and the genuine priceless
masterpiece?

Save it
for a discerning connoisseur
who knows its exquisite beauty
and value

Our ephemeral love
left to exist in its fruition
was a stolen moment
of light and laughter
shown to few
leaving tracks forever

Live loud
Laugh often
Love big

xox,
Wanda

www.ingramcontent.com/pod-product-compliance
Lightning Source LLC
Chambersburg PA
CBHW071322080526
44587CB00018B/3322